THE CURIOUS WORLD OF CRYSTALS

THE CURIOUS WORLD OF CRYSTALS

LENORE SANDER

ILLUSTRATED
BY
JOHN KAUFMANN

PRENTICE-HALL, INC.,
ENGLEWOOD CLIFFS, N. J.

to Larry Wetzel
a fifth grade friend who is
very interested in crystals

another P-H Junior Research Book by Lenore Sander:
Animals that Work for Man

Third printing........February, 1967

The Curious World of Crystals
by Lenore Sander

19558-J

PRENTICE-HALL INTERNATIONAL, INC., *London*
PRENTICE-HALL OF AUSTRALIA, PTY., LTD., *Sydney*
PRENTICE-HALL OF CANADA, LTD., *Toronto*
PRENTICE-HALL OF INDIA (PRIVATE) LTD., *New Delhi*
PRENTICE-HALL OF JAPAN, INC., *Tokyo*

CONTENTS

CHAPTER ONE

CRYSTALS ALL AROUND YOU

Where would you expect to find crystals? In a rock? In a museum? Or perhaps in your mother's jewelry box? Crystals are everywhere. Every day you wear and even *eat* crystals—though you may not see them unless you know what to look for.

If it surprises you to think of wearing and eating crystals, that may be because you are not used to thinking of the metal belt buckles and buttons that you wear, and the salt and sugar that you eat, as being made up of crystals. You will begin to see some of the most familiar things around you in an exciting new way as you learn about crystals. The world of crystals is full of surprises!

Just *what* is a crystal? The word *crystal* comes from a Greek word meaning *clear ice*. At first, only ice itself and clear, colorless rock quartz were called crystals.

7

But in the seventeenth century, when scientists began asking many new questions about everything, the meaning of the word "crystals" came to include many other materials.

These scientists wondered what it was about ice and quartz that made them crystals. They knew many liquids are also clear and colorless, yet no one had ever called them crystals. Besides, rock quartz and ice *act* very differently. When you bring a piece of quartz into a heated room, it doesn't melt into a pool of water, like ice. Rock quartz can only be melted at very high temperatures. These scientists reasoned that either it was wrong to call both the quartz and the ice "crystals," or that there was *something else* about both substances that would supply a reason for lumping them together as crystals.

ROCK QUARTZ

ICE FORMING

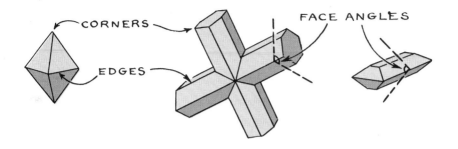

CORNERS

EDGES

FACE ANGLES

As these seventeenth-century scientists studied their samples of rock quartz and watched ice forming under the newly invented microscope, one thing became clear: Both substances take very definite shapes. This, they decided, was what made both of them crystals. So the definition of the word "crystal" opened up to include materials that are colored or colorless, very hard or soft enough to cut with a knife, and easily melted or hard to melt—*as long as they take a definite shape.*

Of course, when these scientists found that crystals take a definite shape, they did not mean that all crystals take the *same* shape. But there are ways in which the shapes of all perfect crystals are alike. They all have flat faces or surfaces. Where two or more of these faces meet, you find angles—or edges and corners.

Once scientists began to study the fascinating forms of crystals, a bright new science was born that is helping to answer some of the most important questions asked

9

STONE

SALT

METAL

by men in almost every other scientific field today. This young science is called *crystallography*—the study of crystals.

The easiest place for you to begin *your* study of crystals is right in your own home. Pour a few grains of salt onto a dark-colored piece of paper, and look at them through a magnifying glass. You will find that the grains are really little cubes, and if you look closely, you may be able to see the flat sides or faces that tell you you are truly looking at crystals.

If any part of your house is made of stone, look at the surface of the stone closely. You will see that each stone is made up of definite shapes all packed together. Again, you are looking at crystals.

10

The crystals that make up metals are harder to see because the smooth surfaces of metals are usually either painted or too shiny for the crystals to show up. However, if you can find a piece of metal that has been broken, and look very carefully at the jagged edge through your magnifying glass, you will see hundreds of the tiny sliver-like crystals that make up the metal.

In your search for crystals, you may come upon a "crystal" punch bowl. "And *that*," you think, "surely is crystal." Well, strange as it may seem, a "crystal" punch bowl is not even made of crystals. Instead, it is made of a fancy kind of glass—and glass is not a *crystalline* material at all.

You may get a clue to the mystery of the punch bowl if you look carefully at a marble that has colors running through it. You probably already know that marbles are made of glass and not of marble. They are called "marbles" because their coloring often resembles that of real marble. But look at those colors carefully. You will see that they are not contained within the definite little

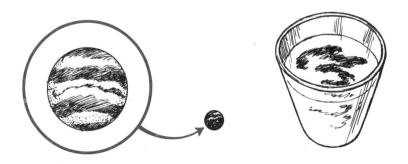

crystal shapes that you can often see very clearly in marble. The colors in a shooter marble follow swirls and seem to blend. If looking at the spirals of color in the *solid* marble makes you think of the way chocolate syrup looks in *liquid* milk before it is stirred, you have found a very important clue to the real secret of glass. But, in order to find out how important your discovery was, we will have to find out *why* solids are solids and liquids are liquids.

CHAPTER TWO THE THREE STATES OF MATTER

Solids, liquids and gases are matter. Glass is made of matter—and so are you. The rocks that build mountains, the water in the oceans and the air around you are matter. Matter is *everything* that makes up the world.

Rocks, water and air are examples of the three *states* that matter takes. As you know, rocks are solids; water is a liquid, and air is a mixture of gases. But what is it that makes one thing a solid, another a liquid, and still another a gas?

One way to throw some light on this question is to look at a kind of matter that can be changed into each of the three states. The most familiar substance that comes in all three states is water—which can be a liquid, or gaseous steam, or solid ice. Let's find out how water, steam and ice *behave* when you pour them from a container of one shape, into a container of another shape.

13

GAS LIQUID SOLID

When you pour liquid water from one container into another of a different shape, you end up with the same amount of water, but the water has taken on the shape of the new container. Therefore, you have found out that liquid water keeps its volume but not its shape.

Now, catch some steam from the teapot in your first container and try to pour it into the second. What do you have? Why, nothing of course. The gas or water vapor has disappeared. So you have shown that this gas has kept neither its volume nor its shape.

Finally, get an ice cube from the refrigerator. Without even trying to put the ice cube in one container and then the other, it will be clear to you that solid ice will keep *both* its volume and its shape.

What you have demonstrated is true of all liquids, solids and gases. Any crystalline substance you put in any container will act as your solid ice did. It will keep its volume and its shape. But so will glass which, although it is solid, is *not* crystalline. It is *amorphous*, which comes from a Greek word meaning *without form*. Scientists refer to all matter which is not crystalline as amorphous. Glass, liquids and gases are amorphous.

But glass is very different from liquids and gases because it is solid. Why, then, is glass not a crystalline substance? Clearly, there is something strange going on here—and it has to do with *molecules*.

As you know, all matter is made up of atoms or arrangements of atoms called molecules. Ice, steam, and water are all made up of exactly the same kind of molecules. But something happens to make the molecules behave differently in different states.

When you put water in a teapot and begin to heat it, the heat *excites* the tiny molecules, and they begin to move faster and faster, until some of them are moving so fast that they keep on going out of the liquid and into the air. As they enter the air they are, like the molecules of the air itself, very far apart from each other and they dash about in a rapid and disordered way. That is why steam seems to disappear when it is mixed with air. The molecules are so small, and have gotten too far apart, for you to see that anything is there.

You have to have millions of molecules all close together in order to see *anything*. A tiny drop of water is made of billions and billions of molecules. At ordinary

15

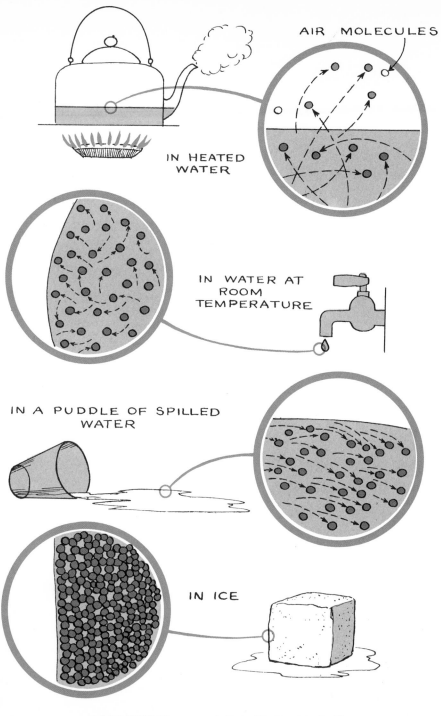

AIR MOLECULES

IN HEATED
WATER

IN WATER AT
ROOM
TEMPERATURE

IN A PUDDLE OF SPILLED
WATER

IN ICE

WATER   MOLECULES

room temperature, the water molecules are not moving nearly so fast as they were in the steam, and they are all clustered together. If there was a microscope powerful enough to see the molecules in a puddle of spilled water, you would see them all tumbling and sliding over each other and jostling their neighbors.

When you make water cold enough for it to start to freeze, something very different begins to happen to the molecules. As the temperature drops, they slow down and begin to take ordered positions—until enough of them have arranged themselves for you to be able to see the solid ice crystal that has formed. In the crystal, a molecule is no longer free to mill around in the crowd, as it was in the liquid. But it hasn't stopped moving altogether. Now it is vibrating in one place, as if it is being held in a little cage.

When glass forms, something peculiar happens. The molecules do not line up and arrange themselves in any definite order, except here and there, quite by accident.

MOLECULES
IN GLASS

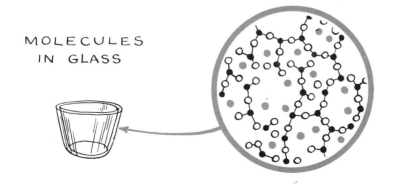

MOLECULES IN COLD SUGAR

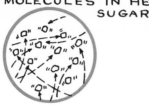
MOLECULES IN HEATED
SUGAR

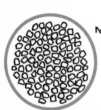
MOLECULES IN
SUGAR GLASS

MELT SUGAR, THEN POUR
ONTO A COLD COOKIE SHEET

MAKING SUGAR GLASS

If you could look at the molecules in glass you would
find that they are like the molecules in a liquid—they are
all jumbled together.

When scientists refer to glass and some other solids
(such as plastics) as amorphous or without form, they
are not describing how these materials *look*. They are
describing the lack of *order* among the molecules. Glass
can be molded into an endless variety of forms, but it
will never take a definite shape by itself. Therefore,
glass and similar solids are *not crystals*—because only
crystals *take a definite form*.

There are many more kinds of this strange solid called
glass than most people suspect. Most glass that you see

18

is made from melted sand. It can also be produced from boric acid, sugar and other things. Glass can be made from any material that is made of *large, unevenly shaped molecules*. When such a material is heated, until it turns into a liquid, and is then cooled quickly—the molecules will have trouble sliding past their neighbors into *ordered* positions. You then have a tangled mass of molecules that are unable to rearrange themselves—in other words, you have *glass*.

You can easily make glass yourself—out of sugar. All you need is about a half cup of sugar and a pan to melt it in. Grease a cookie sheet well, so your glass won't stick to it, and put the sheet into the refrigerator to cool. Heat the sugar very slowly, until it is all melted. As you are doing this, try to imagine how the heat is making all the molecules in the tiny sugar crystals vibrate faster and faster—until they are able to rip open their "cages" and tumble about. When they have all done this, your sugar is melted. Now take the cold cookie sheet and pour your melted sugar onto it. As the cold makes the molecules sluggish and traps them in their flowing liquid confusion, the sugar immediately hardens into a sheet of glass.

CHAPTER THREE PATTERNS IN CRYSTALS

There are no microscopes powerful enough to see the little particles that make up a crystal. But if there were, you could see that all of the tiny atoms or molecules a crystal is built of are arranged in a definite *pattern* that repeats itself over and over throughout the entire crystal.

Imagine laying bricks neatly, side by side and end to end, until you have made a large square. Now think of placing another layer of bricks over the first, so that each brick covers half of two bricks in the first layer. If you went on building layer after layer, you would eventually have constructed a huge cube shape in your imagination. This giant cube would turn out to have an orderliness very much like the order in a perfect crystal. Everywhere in the cube, the bricks would be fitted tightly together, with no empty spaces, or places where the bricks are just jumbled up. If you thought of each brick as a unit, then you would have a structure that is built of repeating units. A crystal is also built of repeating units.

There is another very important way that your cube of bricks would resemble the structure of a crystal. Although the pattern of the bricks would be orderly in all directions, the sort of order would be different in each direction. In other words, if you looked at the structure from one of one pair of sides, you would see a zigzag pattern of *sides* of bricks. If you saw the bricks from one of the other pair of sides, you would see *ends* of the oblong brick shapes. And if you looked at the big brick cube from the top or bottom, you would see only the pattern made by the largest surfaces of the bricks.

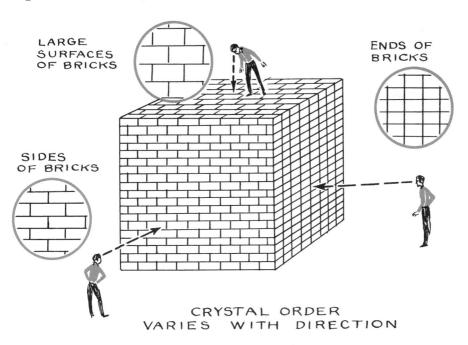

LARGE
SURFACES
OF BRICKS

ENDS OF
BRICKS

SIDES
OF BRICKS

CRYSTAL ORDER
VARIES WITH DIRECTION

The importance of this fact that *crystal order varies with direction* would be made clear to you if you were a giant with a big knife trying to cut through the brick cube you have imagined. If you cut down or up through the cube, you would find it hard going, because you would actually have to cut *through* bricks in every other layer. But if you sliced into the brick cube from the side, between one layer and the next, the knife would slide right in between the bricks. This gives you an idea why you cannot just slice through a crystal any old way. A crystal can be cut—as any diamond cutter would tell you —but it can *only* be cut *between layers*.

Of course it is impossible to *see* the pattern of atoms in a crystal. They are too tiny to be seen even with the most powerful microscope. But today scientists can examine

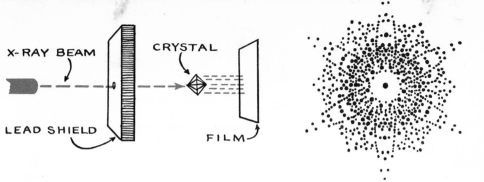

the structure of a crystal in another way. They shoot an X-ray beam at a crystal, directing the beam through a hole in a lead shield. As the beam penetrates, some of the rays are scattered by the tiny atomic particles that make up the crystal. These scattered rays are caught on a piece of film, where they show up as exposed spots. From the pattern of scattering that these spots make on the film, scientists are able to "read" the order in the crystal.

But long before scientists could *prove* that crystals are orderly, thoughtful men had a pretty good idea that they were. They had noticed when they tried to grow crystals that crystalline substances tend to take certain shapes that are characteristic of them. This could only have happened if the building blocks that make up crystals were arranged in some definite kind of order.

Now, when you admire the glittering shapes of the crystals in rocks, you will probably wonder how all that order came about in the first place. This is an interesting thing to wonder about—more interesting, perhaps, than you know. Crystals don't just happen—they *grow.*

23

CHAPTER FOUR

HOW CRYSTALS GROW

When you grow, your body is growing from *inside*. The nutriments in the food that you eat are carried by your blood to all the tiny cells that you are made of, and enables them to multiply so that you grow taller, broader and stronger. Crystals grow differently. They grow from *outside*. The only way for a crystal to grow is for the right kind of atoms or molecules to reach its surfaces and fit themselves into the same pattern of order the tiny "seed" crystal has.

Two things are absolutely necessary for atoms and molecules to get into the ordered places that build a perfect crystal—*time* and *freedom*. The tiny particles have to be able to move freely enough so that they can get into their places on the crystal surface. And they must have enough time to do this. When we talked about glass, we were talking about one of the things that can

24

happen to a collection of molecules that don't have enough time or freedom to get into any real "long" range order. But, given these essential conditions, atoms and molecules can form crystals under some very surprising circumstances.

Can you imagine crystals growing from a gas? Well, strange as it might seem, that is exactly what is happening in the sky above you every winter. Snowflakes grow directly from water vapor, which, as you know, is a gas. In cold weather, the water molecules high up in the air are able to get into the ordered places that produce the tiny, delicately beautiful ice crystals that we call snow.

Crystals can also grow directly from a solid like *tungsten*, a metal which is used to make the filament in light bulbs. When this metal is put under stress and heated very hot—but not hot enough to melt it and turn it into a disordered liquid—it will form large crystals.

Crystals are more commonly grown from a molten or melted substance. Most of the crust of the earth was formed this way. *Geologists*, the scientists who study the

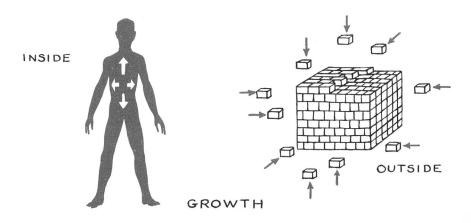

INSIDE

OUTSIDE

GROWTH

earth, think that a very long time ago the entire earth was molten. The heavier molten materials remained at the center of the earth, and the lighter stuff rose to the surface. Then, as the earth cooled, this light, free-floating layer began to build crystals that formed rocks.

Molten material is still boiling up from cracks in the earth's surface and being spat out by volcanoes. This molten mass of lava dissolves already-formed rocks, which crystallize again, and then forms new rocks. This is why such rocks are called *igneous*, which means *formed by fire*. You can recognize an igneous rock, like *basalt*, by the way a freshly-broken surface looks—all jagged and sharp, with many different-shaped little crystal forms sticking up out of it.

If you start searching for crystal forms in rocks, it is very unlikely that you will be able to find perfect ones. The reason for this again has to do with the time and freedom a crystal needs for growth.

A growing crystal will grow as long as the kind of atoms it is made of can reach its surfaces—or until something else gets in its way. With crystals growing from molten materials, the something that gets in the way is usually another crystal. Since crystals are already arranged inside and can only build on their surfaces, there is no possibility of two crystals that have grown toward each other uniting to become one single, perfect crystal. Instead, they just grow until they touch, and then become stuck together—grown together, really. Many crystals, all grown together in this way, are called a *polycrystalline mass.*

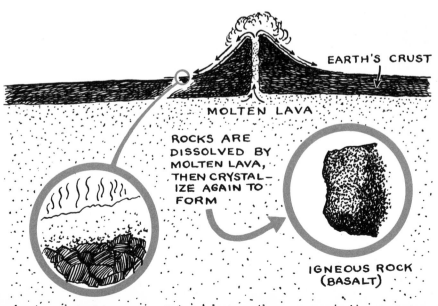

EARTH'S CRUST

MOLTEN LAVA

ROCKS ARE DISSOLVED BY MOLTEN LAVA, THEN CRYSTAL-IZE AGAIN TO FORM

IGNEOUS ROCK (BASALT)

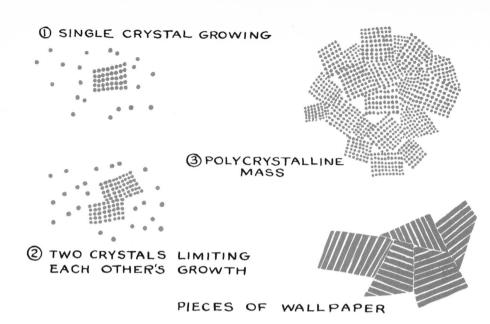

① SINGLE CRYSTAL GROWING

③ POLYCRYSTALLINE
MASS

② TWO CRYSTALS LIMITING
EACH OTHER'S GROWTH

PIECES OF WALLPAPER

In a polycrystalline mass all the stuck-together crystals of the same kind form the same pattern. But the order of the pattern runs in different directions. To understand this better, take a piece of wallpaper with a small repeating pattern on it, and cut it up into several straight-sided pieces. Now, fit the pieces together, not as they were, but any old way, just so that they are edge to edge and do not overlap. You will find that the order of your pattern now runs in several different directions, like the order of the crystals in a polycrystalline mass.

Common metals are all polycrystalline masses, and it is easy to see why when you think about the fact that metals are manufactured by a fairly rapid cooling of molten ores. As the metal cools to the temperature at

28

which it solidifies, millions of little crystals will begin to form all at once. They grow very rapidly, getting into each other's way, and the result is a polycrystalline mass.

Metals are quite hard to handle in the molten state because most metals do not melt unless they are very hot. However, to find out how polycrystalline masses form, there is an experiment you can do with something else.

You will need 25 grams of *salol* (which the chemist calls *phenyl salicylate*). You can get the amount you

GROWING SALOL CRYSTALS

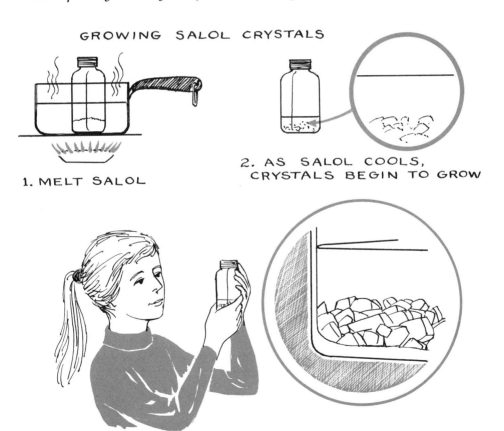

1. MELT SALOL

2. AS SALOL COOLS, CRYSTALS BEGIN TO GROW

need at almost any drugstore, for around a dollar. Ask your druggist to put the salol into a clear glass bottle with flat sides. To melt your salol, put the bottle into a pan of water that is hot, but not boiling. When it is all melted, remove the bottle from the heat, and watch your salol closely through the bottle as it cools. As soon as it has cooled past its melting point, you will be able to see small crystals beginning to grow. Each little crystal will get bigger and bigger until other growing crystals get in its way. You will end up with a mass of crystal shapes all grown together—your own home-grown polycrystalline mass.

Now put your bottle of salol crystals in a safe place— out of reach of younger brothers and sisters, who may not know that it is dangerous to taste anything a scientist is working with. Later, you may find it interesting to compare the way your salol crystals grew from the molten substance, with the way crystals grow from a solution— and it is *solutions* that we are going to talk about next.

CHAPTER FIVE SOLUTIONS

Of all the many ways in which crystals can grow, the easiest way for you to grow them—and in many ways the most interesting—is in a *liquid solution*. Before you start working with a solution, however, there are some very important things that you should know about solutions.

When you dissolve salt in water, you have made a solution. So, you think, a solution is made by dissolving a solid in a liquid. But wait! That's not the whole story by any means. What would you call a gas dissolved in a liquid—like the carbon dioxide gas that makes the soda you drink so fizzy? Yes, you're right. That is a solution, too.

Now we have tried dissolving two of the three states of matter in a liquid and found that we have solutions. What about the other state that matter comes in—the liquid state? Of course, a liquid dissolved in a liquid—like alcohol in water—is a solution too.

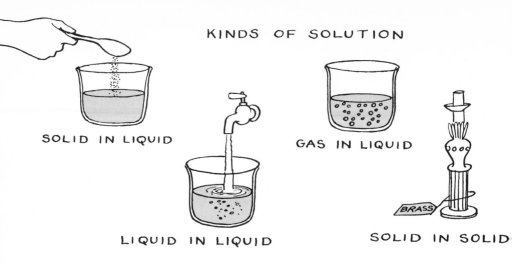

SOLID IN LIQUID

GAS IN LIQUID

LIQUID IN LIQUID

SOLID IN SOLID

But so far, we have only covered *liquid* solutions. There are solutions that have no liquid in them at all. Right now you are breathing such a solution—*air*. The blanket of air, or atmosphere, that makes life on our earth possible, is a solution of several gases.

If you have a pair of brass candlesticks, or a brass lamp, at your house, it is very likely that you have never thought of these objects as solutions. But they are. Brass is a *solid* solution—made by melting copper and zinc together, and then letting them harden. Mixtures of metals like this are called *alloys*, and there are many sorts of alloys made from combinations of metals. So a solution can be made from substances in *any* of the three states of matter, as long as they can be thoroughly mixed.

But the two substances in a solution must be mixed together in particles no larger than a molecule. Milk, for instance, doesn't make the grade as a solution, because the butterfat globules which milk contains come in particles much bigger than any molecule.

Although you can make a solution by dissolving *any amount* of one substance in another substance, there are limits to how much of something WILL dissolve. And these limits can change when you make your solutions hotter or colder.

Have you ever noticed the tiny bubbles of air that start to rise up through water when you begin to heat it? More and more of these little bubbles form and rise to the top as the temperature of the water gets nearer and nearer to the point at which it begins to boil. This is because the heat is making air that is dissolved in the water come *out* of solution. There is a general rule that scientists discovered long ago about this—gases are not as *soluble*, or easily dissolved, in hot liquid as they are in cold liquid. When you heat a solution of any gas in a liquid, the gas will try to escape from the liquid.

However, if you put a certain solid substance—sugar, for instance—into a glass of cold water, *less* of it will dissolve than if you put it in hot water. When you start thinking about molecules and how they behave, it is easy to see why gases and solids generally act differently at the same temperature. You remember that when you make molecules hotter and hotter, they move faster.

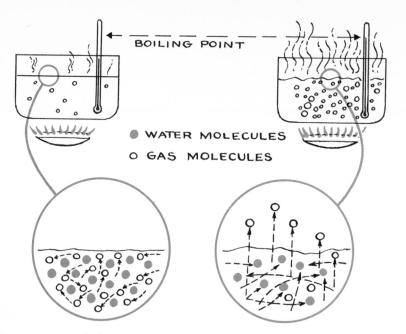

BOILING POINT

● WATER MOLECULES
O GAS MOLECULES

GASES ARE LESS SOLUBLE IN HOT LIQUID THAN IN COLD LIQUID

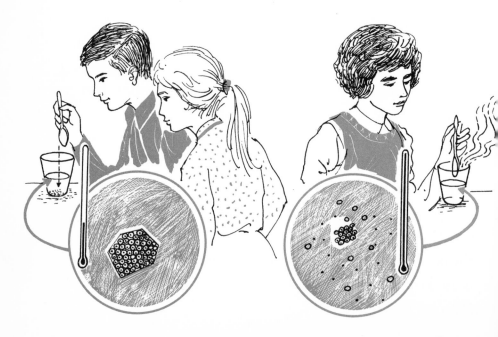

SUGAR MOLECULES ARE MORE SOLUBLE IN HOT LIQUID THAN IN COLD LIQUID

Therefore, when you heat gas molecules that are dissolved in a liquid, the gas molecules try to escape from the crowds of molecules in the liquid. The molecules that make up the liquid also move faster, and are further apart, when they are hot. So, the gas molecules can push their way through the spaces between them, and up into the air where they are able to dash around in almost complete freedom.

But, if you make the molecules of the sugar hotter, they get *more* freedom by escaping into the liquid from the little "cages" in which they were vibrating in the crystals. A rise in temperature gives them the energy to rip open their "cages" so that they can mingle with the crowds of molecules of the liquid.

When all the sugar a glass of water can hold is dissolved, you have a *saturated* solution. No matter how long you wait, no more will dissolve—*at that temperature.*

A solution from which crystals can grow must be *supersaturated*—which means it must contain *more* of the molecules of the dissolved crystalline solid than the liquid can hold. It is only from these *extra* molecules that your crystals will grow. But, how is it possible to get these extra molecules into the solution? Can you think of a way? As you shall soon see, all you have to do is make a saturated solution at a hot temperature, and then let it cool.

CHAPTER SIX GROWING CRYSTALS IN SOLUTION

A crystal grower can "seed" a supersaturated solution with a small crystal of the same substance that is dissolved in his solution. This will very often coax the solution to begin depositing its excess material atom by atom, and molecule by molecule, on the surfaces of the seed—which will then grow larger.

Of course, if the atoms or molecules were just dumped onto the surfaces of the seed crystal, you would end up with an orderless blob. The amazing thing is that they are not. Each little building block neatly positions itself in a definite place, enlarging the same pattern of order that the seed crystal has. So, what results is a larger crystal that has faces, angles and edges, just like those in the seed from which it grew.

If you take your salol crystals out of their hiding place now, you can do an experiment that will show you how

36

crystals can grow when they are in supersaturated solutions. You will also see that your salol crystals will grow much more slowly from a solution than they did when you grew them from the molten substance.

First, go to the drugstore again and ask for 100 *cc* (which stands for *cubic centimeters*) of denatured alcohol. Put the salol crystals and the alcohol together in a closed bottle, keeping a piece of salol crystal in reserve for your *seed*. Now, warm the bottle in hot tap water, and shake it well until the cloudy solution becomes perfectly clear. Allow the solution to cool and become supersaturated. When your solution has cooled, you can drop in your seed. (Be sure the salol and alcohol mixture has completely cooled or the seed will be apt to dissolve, too). Now be patient. You may have to wait two or three days before your crystals grow big enough for you to see them. They will only stop growing when there are no extra molecules left in the liquid solution.

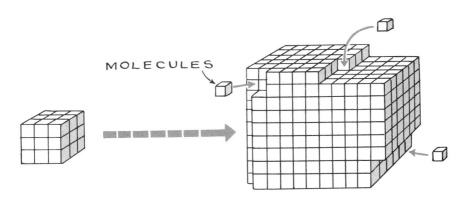

MOLECULES

A SEED CRYSTAL GROWS INTO A LARGE CRYSTAL

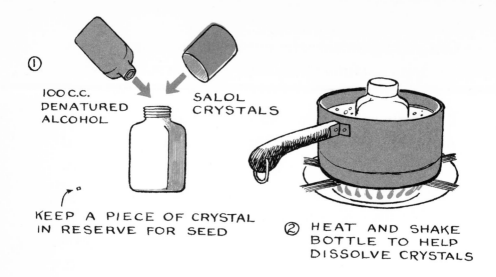

① 100 C.C. DENATURED ALCOHOL

SALOL CRYSTALS

KEEP A PIECE OF CRYSTAL IN RESERVE FOR SEED

② HEAT AND SHAKE BOTTLE TO HELP DISSOLVE CRYSTALS

③ WHEN SOLUTION COOLS, DROP IN SEED CRYSTAL

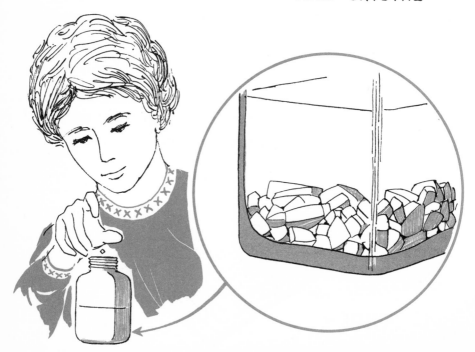

GROWING SALOL CRYSTALS FROM SOLUTION

Can you figure out why crystals grow so much more slowly from a *solution* than from a molten substance? In the molten salol, only salol molecules were tumbling and sliding over each other. No other kinds of molecules were around to interfere with them as they arranged themselves in ordered places in the growing crystals. However, in your solution you have *both* alcohol and salol molecules. So, each salol molecule has to push its way through a crowd of alcohol molecules to get to a place on the surface of the crystal it is helping to build.

As you watch crystals growing from solution, you may wonder *why* each of those billions of molecules moves to an exact place. What makes nature so orderly? Even the most learned scientist cannot answer that question for you. The orderliness in nature is one of the greatest beauties and mysteries of life.

Crystal order is especially mysterious when we think of how much easier it is for matter to become disordered,

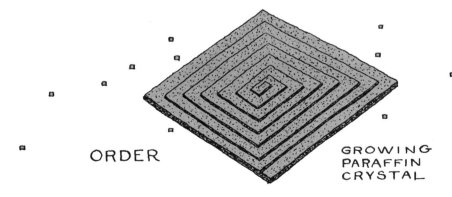

ORDER

GROWING
PARAFFIN
CRYSTAL

DISORDER

DISSOLVING
SALT

than for it to become ordered. The willingness of matter to become disordered is something that scientists have to cope with every day. When a scientist heats a substance to its melting point, nothing that he can do will keep the frisky atoms and molecules from going into the disordered riot of the molten state. When he puts salt into water, he knows that the salt atoms will break free from their "cages" and tumble around in the disorder of the water molecules.

When a scientist tries to *force* nature into orderliness, he really finds out how stubbornly it seems to prefer disorder. The process of attaining orderliness is a slow one. To achieve orderliness in a crystal, millions and millions of little atomic, or molecular, building blocks must move into definite positions in a pattern that grows outward, layer by layer. The wonder is that it happens at all. So, it is not surprising that *disorder* sometimes occurs in the growth of a crystal. Studying these disorders, and discovering the very important uses they can be put to, is one of the most valuable and interesting parts of the crystallographer's work.

CHAPTER SEVEN STOWAWAY ATOMS

Disorder in a crystal is always very limited. You will never find places in a crystal structure where its atomic building blocks are lying around in a jumbled mass. By thinking of these atomic building blocks as bricks, you can get a clear idea of one kind of crystal disorder. If you were going to build a wall, you would buy bricks of the same size and shape. Then as you were building your wall, you would arrange them in a definite pattern of order. It wouldn't change the order if some of the bricks were another color, would it? But you couldn't use any that were not the same size and shape without changing the design of your whole wall, could you?

The same thing is true for a crystal. The *foreign* atoms that a crystal can easily include in its structure must have the same crystal-building *habits* as the other atoms in the structure.

Crystals having this kind of limited disorder are called *mixed crystals*. And some of our most beautiful gemstones are mixed crystals. Two of the most valuable gems there are, the *sapphire* and the *ruby*, are built from molecules made up mostly of aluminum and oxygen atoms. Here and there, *foreign* molecules have fitted themselves into the structure. It is these substituted molecules that give such precious stones their beautiful colors.

Sometimes even an atom that is not at all like the other atoms in a crystal can slip into the structure and get away with it. Not very many of these stowaway atoms can be hidden in the crystal—only one, say, for every million regular atoms. This is not a very common defect, but it is a very important one.

Just a few years ago, vacuum tubes began to be replaced by tiny *transistors*, made of crystals. Transistors are smaller than the smallest vacuum tube that can be made, but they do the job of amplifying and switching electrical signals much better than the old tubes. They also do not have to be replaced constantly, and operate perfectly well in the midst of vibrations and shocks that would knock out old-style vacuum tubes. If you have watched our astronauts taking off into space, you will understand how important *that* is in the electrical systems of spaceships!

There are people walking around today who owe the fact that they are alive to tiny machines embedded in the flesh of their bodies that give electrical signals to their hearts to keep them beating. These miniature machines, called *pacemakers*, work because they are powered by transistors.

The huge computers that solve complicated mathematical problems in the wink of an eye contain thousands of tiny transistors. Telephone systems, pocket radios, and just about every other electrical machine that has become smaller and more efficient, use transistors.

The fabulous transistor is really a crystal—a very special three-part structure made of *germanium* and *silicon* crystals. What makes these crystals so special is that they

FOREIGN ATOM
SUBSTITUTING FOR
A REGULAR ATOM

SAPPHIRE

RUBY

FOREIGN ATOM
HIDING BETWEEN
REGULAR ATOMS

STOWAWAY ATOMS MAKE "MIXED CRYSTALS"

have been "doped," which means they have stowaway arsenic and gallium atoms embedded in their crystal structures. These stowaway atoms are responsible for what the scientist calls *n-Type* and *p-Type defects,* that enable the three crystal parts to handle an electrical impulse in the varied ways that make the transistor so useful.

Crystallographers have recently presented still another advance to the world of electronics. It is an even tinier crystal that is able to do the same work as the transistor. Already a midget computer called UNIVAC 1824 is using these miniscule crystals. This miniature computer only weighs seventeen pounds! Because it is so light and small, UNIVAC 1824 is being used as an automatic pilot in satellites and spaceships.

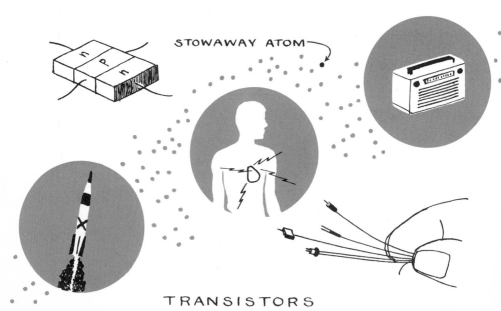

STOWAWAY ATOM

TRANSISTORS

The crystallographer has become a very important man in the world of science. His work helps men in almost every other branch of science find answers to some of the most puzzling questions. *Metallurgists,* scientists who study metals, have been helped by crystallographers to understand another kind of crystal defect that is very important.

For a long time, metallurgists wondered why certain types of crystals grew when all the rules said they would not. Crystallographers were able to explain to them that one of the problems met by people who grow crystals is that when one layer on a crystal face is completed, the crystal will often stop growing. This is because not enough of the atoms in the vapor, or liquid surrounding the crystal, can arrive at the same time to get a new layer started. When only a few tiny atoms can manage to get into places, there aren't enough other atoms ready to go into places around them to hold them there. So the few that have settled take off again, and the crystal doesn't grow. But sometimes the crystal *does* grow in spite of this.

The crystallographer calls such growth a *screw-type dislocation.* This kind of growth occurs when all the atoms in the first layer do not put themselves together on the same level or plane, and a section of the first layer has become raised.

45

NEW ATOMS ALIGHT
ON THE EDGE OF
THE STEP...

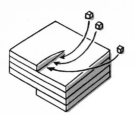

CAUSING THE STEP
TO GROW AND
ROTATE

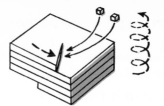

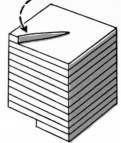

THE CRYSTAL GROWS
LAYER BY LAYER IN
AN UPWARD SPIRAL

SCREW-TYPE DISLOCATION

Such crystals keep presenting their uneven step surfaces for new atoms to light on. These atoms stay to finish another strange uneven surface for the next layer to grow on. So the step-like structure continues to grow in a spiral, layer by layer.

There are many other kinds of dislocations, some of which explain why certain metals can be stretched and bent without breaking. Few things are more interesting than these dislocations—or more useful in making crystals do the jobs the crystallographer wants them to do.

Even an imperfect crystal is one of the most orderly things in nature. Glass, plastics, and water will sometimes show a spot of order that has come about by chance. But crystals exhibit long stretches of beautifully aligned atomic building blocks, and it is rare to find even *one* in several thousand out of line.

Although we cannot see the order inside a crystal without elaborate equipment and the special training of the modern crystallographer, we *can* take a look at the *outside order* of crystals. And, if you look at crystal shapes, as the earliest crystallographers did, you will be surprised at how much there is to think about.

CHAPTER EIGHT CRYSTAL SHAPES

The shimmering beauty of a perfect crystal is a wonderful thing for anyone to see, and the variety of crystal shapes has long fascinated men of science. Crystal shapes gave scientists the first key that helped to unlock the mysteries of crystalline matter.

How do you suppose an early scientist would have gone about learning something from his collection of crystals? He would have started searching for something that all the crystals in his collection had in common. Just looking at them, he could have seen that all of them had flat faces and edges and corners that formed angles. He could have given a general description of all his crystals by saying that they were all *polyhedra,* meaning that they were all figures bounded by a definite number of faces.

But what next? Well, his next step would have been to start *measuring* his crystals. Then he would have compared these measurements and looked for a *relationship* —something similar in his measurements, that would tell him more about his crystals.

Fortunately, the angles in crystals can be measured and compared by using a simple instrument called a *goniometer*, which has two jaws. A seventeenth-century Danish doctor, Nicolaus Steno, used this instrument, and with it he made a very important discovery. He found that when a crystal has pairs of faces that are shaped alike, the angles between these faces are *always the same*. This is true of any crystal, no matter whether it is large or small. With this discovery, he took the first step toward understanding crystals.

A century later, another giant step was taken when two Frenchmen, named Rome de Lisle and Abbé René Just Haüy, were also measuring the angles of crystals. They found out that the angles between crystal faces of the *same substance* are always the same. Things can happen to the *shapes* of crystals of the same substance that make them look very different, but the angles between

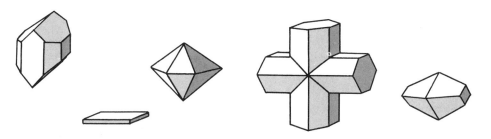

POLYHEDRA

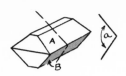

IF FACES A AND B
ARE SIMILAR IN SHAPE
TO FACES C AND D,
THEN ANGLE α EQUALS
ANGLE b

STENO'S
GONIOMETER
(OPENS TO MEASURE
ANY ANGLE)

NICOLAUS STENO

ABBÉ HAÜY

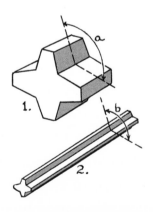

IF ANGLE α EQUALS
ANGLE b, THEN CRYSTALS
1 AND 2 ARE OF THE
SAME SUBSTANCE

their faces will always be the same. For instance, it is possible to have a long, thin crystal and a short, fat crystal of the same substance—if something happened to one of the crystals while it was growing. So, even though both crystals are made of the same kind of atoms, and put together in the same order, they don't *look* like the same kind of crystal. But they *are the same inside*. Measuring the angles between pairs of faces on both the short and the long crystals will *prove* that they are alike.

Even today, when a chemist has a crystal that he cannot identify, he will measure its angles and then compare these measurements with records of the measurements of known crystals. If he finds a substance in the records that has exactly the same angles as his unknown crystal, he will then know that they are both the same substance.

Studying the angles in crystals, crystallographers made yet another discovery—perhaps the most important of all, in understanding crystalline matter. They found that the exact kind of angle that a given crystal species has as its trademark is always built by a *particular kind of building block*. In other words, the kinds of angles that identify a particular crystalline substance tell you the *shape* of its building blocks. Just think for a moment about the importance of *that* discovery!

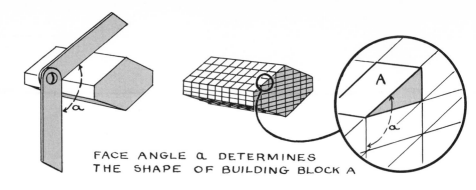

FACE ANGLE α DETERMINES
THE SHAPE OF BUILDING BLOCK A

Men did not always know that matter was made up of atomic and molecular particles. It was not very many centuries ago that most scientists thought that matter was *continuous*. They believed that one could *continue* to cut up a tiny piece of matter over and over again, and never get to the point where there would be anything but a *tinier* piece of the *same* matter.

Of course, today we know that matter is *discontinuous,* and that when we examine matter in tinier and tinier pieces, a point is reached where we find the *discontinuous* particles from which that matter is built. Of course, you know that matter is discontinuous because you know that everything is made of atoms and molecules. But, can you imagine the value the discovery that crystals are discontinuous substances made up of tiny units was to scientists? Added to this, they also discovered that measuring the angles of crystal faces helped them make an educated guess about the *shape* of the tiny, unseen blocks that form crystal structures.

CHAPTER NINE CHANGING "HABITS"

The characteristic shape a substance takes when it forms a crystal is called its *habit*. Left completely alone, with plenty of time and freedom, a crystal will follow its habit of growth and become a perfectly formed example of its kind. But there are factors that can keep a growing crystal from following its habit.

You met one of these factors when we talked about the growth of polycrystalline masses. Your growing salol crystals got in each other's way, and none of them had the chance to become perfect single crystals.

When a crystal grows in a supersaturated solution, it takes its building material from the parts of the solution that bathe its faces. So the solution around the crystal becomes lighter and begins to rise, and heavier solution laden with fresh crystal-building material flows into the area to take its place. The constant exchanges of "used

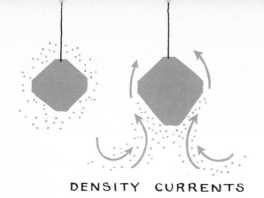

DENSITY CURRENTS

JAR BOTTOM CUTS
OFF CRYSTAL GROWTH

up" solution and fresh solution around a growing crystal are called *density currents*. Such currents can cause an unevenness in the growth of crystal faces, leaving the finished crystal looking a little lopsided.

Also, crystals that are grown in a solution often become deformed. If a "seed" or small crystal is just dropped into a jar full of supersaturated solution, usually the little seed crystal falls on its largest face, and that face is unable to grow—since it is resting against the bottom of the jar where no building materials can get to it. So, after the rest of the crystal has grown for a while, you will have an imperfect crystal with a large, flat, undeveloped face.

There are also ways that the shape of a crystal can be changed after it has stopped growing. You can find a multitude of such changed crystal shapes on a beach— shapes that have been ground smooth by water and wind, and by grinding against one another. The sand itself is a collection of such changed crystals. The pebbles on the beach were once jagged masses of crystal shapes all stuck together. But years and years of being tossed about in the ocean have rubbed them smooth, too.

The enormous pressures that the crust of the earth exerts on the crystals that help form it can bring about distortions of crystal shapes as well. Changes of temperature can also cause certain alterations in crystal structures.

Nothing is a better example of the many ways that nature can change crystal structures than marble. Marble is made up of tiny grains of *calcite*, fitted together in a mosaic that is entirely composed of crystals. And yet there are some types of marble in which you would be hard put to find any definite crystal shapes. The

crystals have been crushed, and massive sections of the stone have been folded in on themselves, sometimes giving the appearance of growth rings on a tree. Alternations of heat and cold have cracked the marble, and molten substances have flowed into the cracks, and crystallized out again, in this confined space. Fitting into a confined space distorts the shapes of the crystals and can give the marble a veined look. The interesting story of the kinds of violence done by weather, temperature and pressure to crystal shapes can be read in almost any stone.

A change in temperature and pressure can have a very surprising effect on certain crystalline substances, too. In these cases, it is not just a matter of a crystal being *deformed*—it is *transformed*.

One substance that behaves in this peculiar way is *phosphorus*. Phosphorus atoms can arrange themselves to form crystals that are either red, white, or black! And

CALCITE GRAINS

VEINED MARBLE

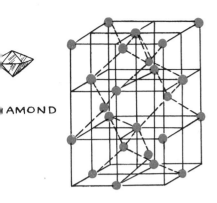

DIAMOND

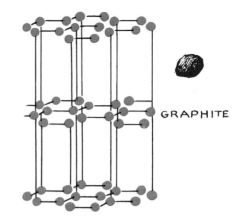

GRAPHITE

as if that isn't strange and mysterious enough, one crystalline form and color of phosphorus can actually be transformed into another. Also, the white form of phosphorus has *two* crystal habits, rather than just one.

If *white* phosphorus crystals are heated in a closed container for a long time, they will turn into *red* phosphorus crystals. Also, if you subject *white* phosphorus crystals to enormous pressures, they will change into *black* phosphorus crystals. All these colors of phosphorus crystals are made up of the *same* kind of atoms. It is their weird ability to put themselves together in such different types of crystal order that has led scientists to call phosphorus an *allotropic* substance—which means that it comes in more than one crystal form.

Another basic kind of substance that shows allotrophy is *carbon*. Two kinds of crystal structures can be formed by carbon atoms, and both occur quite naturally in the

57

crust of our earth. Carbon atoms can put themselves together under normal pressures and temperatures to form a rather soft, gray type of crystal, called *graphite*. However, the crystals carbon forms at high pressures and temperatures, are very different. They are *diamonds*— and diamonds are the hardest known substance. Synthetic diamonds are made by putting graphite under very high pressure and heat. But, fortunately for jewelers, and for your mother too, if she has a diamond ring—it takes an enormously long time to convert a diamond back to graphite, even after the pressure is removed!

CHAPTER TEN GROWING SUGAR CRYSTALS

One of the simplest but most rewarding ways to grow crystals is from sugar, and the best way to be absolutely sure that you will succeed is to get a candy thermometer to measure the temperature of your sugar solution. Then you will know for *sure* when your solution is hot enough to accept an amount of sugar that will yield a very supersaturated solution when it is cooled.

To make your sugar solution, carefully measure two cups of sugar into one cup of water in a pan. Now heat the solution, measuring the temperature with your candy thermometer until the mercury line has gone up to 242 degrees Fahrenheit. If you cannot possibly get a candy thermometer, another not quite so accurate way of judging the temperature of your solution, is to drop a tiny bit of it from time to time into some cold water, as you are heating the mixture. When the drops form a soft ball you will know that the solution is hot enough.

Now remove the solution from the heat and allow it to cool. When it has become quite cool pour the mixture into a tall, thin glass jar.

To follow the next steps (shown on the diagram), you will need a piece of string long enough to reach from the top to the bottom of your glass jar. You will also need a ruler. Tie one end of your string to the middle of the ruler, and the other to a paper clip or a safety pin.

Drop the weighted end of the string (with the paper clip), into your supersaturated sugar solution, making sure that the string does not touch the bottom of the glass. Place the ruler so that the middle of it is centered over the mouth of the jar with the two ends sticking out. This will hold the arrangement in place. The string will give the sugar crystals an uneven surface on which to grow.

Now put the jar of solution someplace where it will not be disturbed or subjected to changes of temperature. It will probably take your sugar crystals several days to grow about an inch.

If you follow directions carefully you will have the satisfaction of growing your own beautiful crystals. You will also have the satisfaction of being able to *eat* your sugar crystals—since another name for your sugar crystals is *rock candy*.

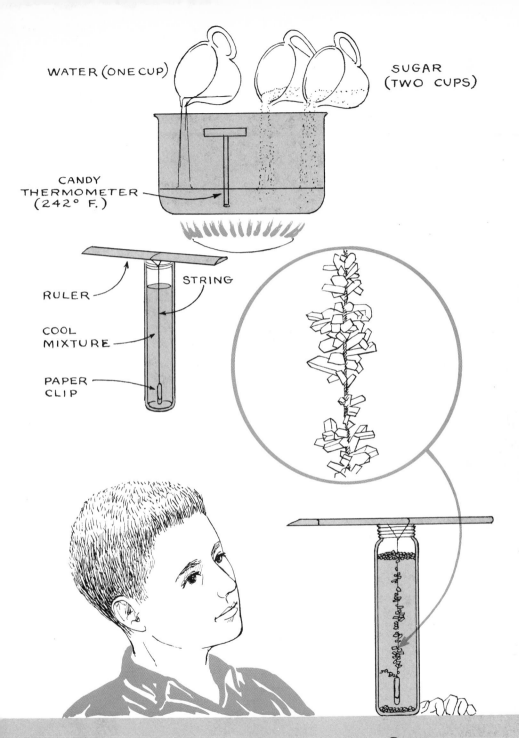

WATER (ONE CUP)

SUGAR
(TWO CUPS)

CANDY
THERMOMETER
(242° F.)

RULER

STRING

COOL
MIXTURE

PAPER
CLIP

GROWING   SUGAR   CRYSTALS

Making rock candy is an easy and interesting way to begin crystal growing. Modern crystallographers spend many, many years attempting to get complex substances to crystallize. Success in growing a few tiny crystals (not even enough to cover the head of a pin) might not sound very important, but some of the most recent advances in science have resulted from just such hard-won successes.

Crystallography has come a long way from its beginnings in the dusty candlelit laboratories of seventeenth-century scientists. Still, there are a great many unanswered questions left for your generation of scientists to investigate in the curious world of crystals.

INDEX